All images contained within this book are the property of Karen Harvey.

Cover image is Quebex's Warlord aged 9 months.

ISBN 978-0-9561492-0-6

Copyright © 2009 by Quebex.
All rights reserved.

THE ROTTWEILER

SUCCESSFUL REARING FROM PUPPYHOOD

Quebex Rottweilers
www.quebex.co.uk

About the Author

Harlem, Karen and Jeno

Karen Harvey was born in Lambeth, London in 1963. From an early age she has shown a natural affinity for dogs, and has been involved with Rottweilers specifically since 1987.

She considers her life with her Rottweilers a journey, and counts herself privileged to have had deep, mutually beneficial relationships with a number of distinguished and fine examples of this noble breed.

As a responsible breeder, she has earned the respect of her peers for her ethical, sympathetic approach to producing healthy, happy, well-balanced dogs, in perfect harmony with both their natural inclinations and the domestic, human-dominated world that they must inhabit.

However, perhaps the biggest indicator of her success is the reciprocal nature of her relationships, in which humankind co-exists with canine in harmony, understanding, trust, and a deep, nurturing love.

By David Hill

My Dedication

I dedicate this book to the memory of my Grandfather who I miss very much. To my partner David, who has inspired me to finally sit down and write it, and with whom I feel complete. And to all my canine friends, past and present, who have touched my life with their innocence, companionship, patience and wisdom and without whom, ultimately, I would not have had the ability and privilege to make this journey.

"You will always be with me, for you are embedded in my heart and I have truly been honoured to share my life with you, each and every one"

Beauty, Ability and Strength

"He, who by understanding, becomes converted to the gospel of service......will serve kindness so that brutality will perish...And, he who is strong, will serve the weak that they may become strong. He will devote his strength, not to the debasement and defilement of his weaker fellows, but to the making of opportunity for them to make themselves into men rather than into slaves and beasts."

From Call of the Wild
By Jack London

CONTENTS
Part 1

1. Introduction.
2. The Rottweiler's Origins
3. Understanding the Rottweiler's Instincts
4. Mother Knows Best.
5. Stages of Development in the Rottweiler.
6. The Needs of a Rottweiler-Follower or Leader.
7. Learn to understand and think like your Rottweiler
8. A Dog or a Bitch?
9. Rescuing a Rottweiler
10. Rottweilers and Children

Part 2
How to be seen as the Leader by your Rottweiler.

Start as you mean to go on and be consistent with Rules and Boundaries.

1. Control
2. Educate the Family
3. Patience
4. Walking Your Rottweiler
5. Grooming and Handling
    a) *Teeth*
    b) *Ears*
    c) *Nails*
    d) *Eyes*
    e) *Coat*
6. Sharing Affection
7. Clear Communication
8. Corrections and Consequences
9. Praise and Acknowledgement
10. Playtime
11. Pack Dynamics
12. Aggression

Time to Decide - *(are you ready to be an ambassador for the Rottweiler?)*
Other Tools You will find Useful - *(a few tools which I think will be helpful)*
A Place for Your Rottweiler's Personal Information - *(a place for important information about your Rottweiler)*
Notes - *(a place to make notes about your Rottweilers training or behaviour for example)*
Other Recommended Reading - *(some of the books which I have read and have inspired me along the way).*
Support this Wonderful Breed

My Rottweilers and Pugs live in harmony.

1. Introduction

For more than twenty years I have had the honour of sharing my life and home with the noblest of breeds - the Rottweiler, and more recently, the Pug. And so it saddens me deeply when I hear the Rottweiler described as a 'Devil Dog', amongst other things, which is a description that could not be further from the truth. When a person has taken the time and effort to educate themselves in the workings of a dog's mind and most importantly the Rottweilers, and understanding this breed's characteristics, they truly are a wonderful animal with which to share your life.

If you love your dog and have its reputation and best interests at heart you have a responsibility to ensure that you acquire the knowledge and tools to educate your Rottweiler in a way that it can best understand. This means learning about them as an *animal first* and this, in turn, makes their life in a human world far easier and much less stressful. It also keeps them safe from persecution. This breed is certainly not suitable for everyone. It requires a home where its needs are met by someone who has the time for training, exercise and socialisation. Such a person must be absolutely committed to raising a well-balanced Rottweiler that people will admire whether in public or at home.

We, as humans, are the ones who must hold ourselves responsible for our dog's behaviour and that applies to ALL breeds! You may be surprised to learn that the majority of dog owners have absolutely no idea what the Dangerous Dog Act is or how it could affect them. Many who have heard of it likely think that the word 'dangerous' only applies to the dog that bites however, a dog who has been allowed to jump up at humans could be classed as dangerous if it injured a small child or a frail and elderly person by jumping up at them. You may see it as being friendly however the law may not! Below is an extract taken from the 'Dangerous Dog Act 1991', which I consider to be particularly relevant but I would strongly recommended that you make yourself familiar with the whole of the Act by looking it up on the internet. You will then see for yourself how it can and does affect <u>every</u> dog owner.

3. Keeping Dogs under Proper Control

(1) If a dog is dangerously out of control in a public place -

(a) The owner; and

(b) If different, the person for the time being in charge of the dog,

Is guilty of an offence, or, if the dog while so out of control injures any person, an aggravated offence, under this subsection."

The above is a small part of the Dangerous Dog Act and applies to all breeds of dog and could be applied to you, even if your Rottweiler simply knocks someone over by being overly friendly. It is your job to protect the Rottweiler in your care by being in charge and taking responsibility for behaviours good or bad, even if it means admitting that you got it wrong. A famous quote by popular TV psychologist 'Dr. Phil' *"You cannot change what you do not acknowledge"*. Oh how true this is.

My biggest concern has always been that as a society we humanise our pets by giving them a name and free run of our homes without really thinking about or knowing the catastrophic results of doing so. Dogs think on a dog's level and have no ability to rationalise like a human can. A dog lives 'in the now' and my belief is that unless you understand the primeval instincts of the Rottweiler in your home, how can you possibly communicate with it on a level that will make any sense?

And so I hope that this book will help you to think *animal first*, and therefore give your Rottweiler the best chance possible to find balance by giving you an insight into what makes a good pack leader, and how you and your chosen Rottweiler, puppy or adult, can make a balanced pack. My aim also is that this book may help you to decide whether the Rottweiler is the right breed of dog for you and your family; and for it to be a handy reference in times when you are perhaps unsure of what to do, or need encouragement or inspiration in raising your Rottweiler to be a balanced and an admired part of our society.

A well behaved Rottweiler is a sure sign that it is part of a balanced pack and follows a worthy human leader.

A badly behaved Rottweiler is a sure sign of your lack of understanding and poor leadership knowledge.

Which one would you like to be described as?

2. The Rottweiler's Origins

The Rottweiler is an ancient breed and is an animal which was believed to have been bred originally to assist Roman soldiers in their movement of cattle when in campaigns of war. The soldier's food was "on the hoof" and so would need to be "*driven*" from place to place by these dogs. These dogs would also have needed the stamina and strength to trot for sometimes hundreds of miles. Another task would also have been to guard the herd from unwanted intruders, human or otherwise, who may have wanted to prey on the cattle which was meant for the Roman soldiers.

This animal looked nothing like the breed we see today but more mastiff-like and less refined; and over the years we have "mixed and matched" looks and capability to achieve what we know as the

"Rottweiler" of today. At one time they were also known as the Butcher's Dog and would pull carts laden with meat for sale. The butcher would put the money from these sales into a pouch which was hung around his Rottweiler's neck for safe keeping.

The name 'Rottweiler' comes from a town in Germany, *Rottweil*, and is where the breed we know today was finally established. Rottweiler means *"red tile"*, a description of the roof covering traditionally used in the town. It is a breed of dog that over the years has seen changes of use within society, from herding, guarding, and pulling of carts, until now, when this animal is most likely seen as a companion that was, and is capable of so much more.

The general appearance of the Rottweiler should be an above average size and stalwart dog, with a correctly proportioned, compact and powerful form. This should permit great strength, manoeuvrability and endurance.

The general characteristics of the Rottweiler should display boldness and courage. Be self assured and fearless, with a calm gaze that should indicate good humour.

The temperament of the Rottweiler should be good natured, not nervous, or aggressive, nor vicious. This dog should be courageous, biddable and possess a natural; guarding instinct – *requirements of the UK Kennel Club Breed Standard.*

We humans have bred dogs over the years to do jobs and fill compartments which have suited us. So when we then take away these jobs, and the dogs become frustrated and bored because they are no longer fulfilled, responsibility surely has to lie at our door for the outcome of such ventures. It seems we are happy to take full responsibility for the good, but not so for the bad.

3. Understanding a Rottweiler's Instincts

Instinct-*the inborn tendency to behave in a particular way without the need for thought.*

Today's Rottweilers are the product of many hundreds of years of breeding and cross-breeding in order to achieve what has been ultimately desired, a breed of dog that should be uniform black and tan, can trot for great distances, has a powerful and strong frame and one that has high levels of confidence and a strong guarding instinct. This breed of dog should also be versatile, friendly and companionable to its master and its extended family.

A Rottweiler puppy is born with a genetic pre-disposition to certain instinctual behaviours which will compel it to react in a particular way given different situations or stimuli. It is my opinion that these instincts, perhaps more commonly known as "drives" are in fact in all breeds of dog but to a higher or lower level, depending on the breed's ultimate purpose of original breeding. Prey, Pack, Flight and Fight instincts are responsible for the decisions our Rottweiler makes in today's world, and to give you a better understanding of what I mean by this I will try and explain what each drive motivates in our dogs.

Prey/Chase Instinct: Chasing of anything that moves, biting, stalking, scenting, hunting, herding and pouncing with the ultimate goal being to catch prey. Watch a puppy chase leaves blowing in the wind or shred a soft toy, or an adult chasing a ball that has been thrown. Prey drive is the instinctive behaviour of a carnivore to chase and capture prey. How do we compel a greyhound to race? We mimic prey by using a stuffed fake rabbit on a track which will be moved at high speed. The greyhound only runs because it is a breed of dog (sight hound) that has a high prey instinct. It is built into its make-up and sometimes we heighten and control these instincts to get a particular behaviour that we want.

Pack/Unit Instinct: A motivation to be within a pack - dog or human, enjoyment of touch and affection, a need to reproduce, a liking of being groomed and to have company. A dog needs to be part of a hierarchy within a pack which would include following rules and boundaries which have been put in place to maintain control and balance.

Fight/Defence Instinct: A dog who is defensive or displays aggression in stressful situations or when challenged. Dominant posturing and standing its ground or the guarding of toys, food or territory and also the enjoyment of confrontational games like tug of war or being possessive, is a dog's desire to self-preserve. A good police dog would have to have a high degree of compulsion to use this instinct and would be encouraged to do so, using correct training by its handler. This behaviour then would be used to ward off criminals or control crowds at a football match for example. A dog that may see a threat to its pack or territory may become defensive and protective of it.

Flight/Avoidance Instinct: Runs away from confrontation, a dog that lacks confidence will use this instinct when unsure, confronted or scared. If this dog is not given the chance to become calm and submissive, or is unable to run away because it may be on a lead or cornered, is very likely to switch to a fight/defence instinct in order to drive away what it fears. Watch for the person who will pick up their "toy dog" when being approached by a larger dog. This small dog is often forced to use defensive behaviour to repel what it has been led by its owner to believe is a threat.

The Rottweiler possesses all of the above instincts in varying degrees, depending on individual personality and lifestyle. A breeder should be able to see these characteristics in the male and female who will ultimately parent the litter. Consequently they should watch how each pup develops within the nest, and how they display each genetic compulsion. The choices which are then made for the future homes of these puppies should be based upon these observations. This is more likely to ensure that each puppy will be placed safely and successfully with a capable owner of the correct lifestyle and experience.

All these instincts are perfectly natural and displayed by all dogs at some level throughout their lives and in various situations. When these instincts are understood and harnessed by a knowledgeable breeder or owner, they can be used to produce a Rottweiler with a stable and reliable temperament. As a new owner you must make it your job to understand what your dog's language is, if you want to safeguard your Rottweiler and its reputation as a breed. A correctly matched, biddable Rottweiler, led by a proud leader is really a pleasure to see.

4. Mother Knows Best

The role of follower in a pack is the state of mind a puppy is born with. From day one their mother displays leadership and will offer discipline and boundaries when and where she feels they are needed. She will correct a behaviour which she does not appreciate and she would not allow boundaries to be crossed unchallenged because it is her job to maintain control. She will not 'punish' a puppy but will give the puppy a consequence for a disagreeable behaviour. This may be a simple nudge or a nip, or she may hold the puppy down using her paw or mouth, but most importantly, all of these consequences would be carried out with a mindset and energy that is worthy of a leader. There would be no room for sympathy or empathy. Any discipline we give to our Rottweiler should always be done in a calm and firm manner and at the moment the unwanted behaviour happens, because dogs 'live in the now'.

If your pup urinates on the carpet and you notice it five minutes later, there would be no point in chastising the pup because it will have no idea what you are trying to tell it. You will in fact confuse the pup and consequently it will have learnt nothing but to be apprehensive of you.

Remember, the more you compound a negative state of mind the less confident your Rottweiler will become, and this is when we find that problems in temperament may occur. Only correct a dog or puppy when you catch it *"in the act"*

For trust to evolve between you and your Rottweiler, <u>never</u> lose your temper. Because losing your temper means that you are not in control and will demonstrate to the dog that you are weak. This will also be seen by the pup/adult Rottweiler as a negative state of mind and it may be taken advantage of.

Your Rottweiler puppy or adult does not take it personally if you have to administer discipline or corrections when appropriate. It will, in fact, learn that you are a very powerful force and energy, and will revere and respect you all the more for it.

When you are consistent and fair and use a calm, controlled state of mind your bond will be that much stronger because you have shown great control of yourself and any situation you may be in.

In my opinion it is a responsible breeder's job to continue the leadership that the puppy's mother has set into place. All puppies are cute and have a need to be nurtured, but without the correct balance of discipline and boundaries they will continue their journey in our world and grow up with an unbalanced state of mind.

Once the puppies are weaned, the breeder should become the disciplinarian, and consequently, their leader. The breeder should then explain to you about their experiences with the litter and particularly the puppy that has been chosen for you. This then will give you a better understanding of <u>why</u> this particular pup is the right one for you and your family and also how the pack (litter) dimensions have worked. I say *chosen* because if you are not experienced in this breed, you may inadvertently pick the puppy whose intensity may be incorrect and not compatible for your family or circumstances. Each puppy will have a slightly different energy and personality. Their behaviour should be observed by the breeder who should be able to choose a puppy with the right type of disposition for your family and environment.

Mother with her pups on day eleven. She shows her litter what a balanced energy feels like. Pups sense energy from the time they are born.

All puppies are born with their own personality and level of instinct and experience their first weeks of our world and their life by using only their nose to find food, warmth and safety.

Their eyes are still developing, as are their ears and these senses will remain shut for around the first 11-14 days after they are born. Their sense of smell is what guides them about the nest, to food and to their mothers' safe and calm energy.

The next senses they master are their eyes and ears. Once opened, they continue to develop until the puppy is about 4 weeks old, at which time a healthy pup should have good vision and hearing.

So my point is that puppies are learning what they are living by *using their nose* to investigate their surroundings - and this is the sense that is of primary use throughout their lives. They use their nose to investigate what type of energy a person, an environment or another dog has at any given time.

This is an important thing to remember if you are to be a successful pack leader because it can tell you a lot about your dog's behaviour and what it is likely to be in a given situation.

When a dog sniffs a visitor, another dog, or you, they are discovering the energy/emotional state being emitted. Their behaviour will be based on what they discover about the body language and individual scent and energy at that particular time. So next time your Rottweiler is sniffing you or a visitor to your home, think about what message may be being received by your dog. His behaviour will tell you. Watch closely!

The correct behaviour to use when being greeted by a dog with an overly excited energy is to ignore the dog until it, and the atmosphere, has become calm. It is then you who must instigate contact by perhaps then calling the dog over to you. This then encourages the dog to exhibit calm behaviours in this circumstance, instead of a stressed and overly excitable one, by your rewarding the correct state of mind in the dog. All visitors should be encouraged by you to not touch, talk to or give eye contact to a dog when introductions occur. This then gives the dog time to calm down and see that your guests are higher ranking than it and must be respected.

Look at the scenario above, and ask yourself who would be in control by following this example? Is it the dog, or is it the human? The message that the dog should receive is that humans are to be respected because it is we who should ultimately control the dog's reactions by displaying vital leadership skills, showing control and calm assertive reactions.

5. Stages of development in the Rottweiler.

Any encounter, good or bad, that your Rottweiler puppy or adult experiences will have an effect on its mental growth, and will dictate how it will respond to that stimulus in the future. The Rottweiler puppy should be socialised correctly, especially while going through critical stages of development. This, in due course will help with the way in which your Rottweiler deals with life's experiences.

The first few weeks of life should be dealt with by the breeder but by the time the pup is ready to leave the nest, at approximately 7-8 weeks of age, you, as the new leader should know the following:

Between the ages of 3-7 weeks the first phase of imprinting (*canine and human awareness*) or socialisation will start, with the brain developing rapidly now, sound and visual socialisation is a must, if disturbances (*fear*) to unfamiliar stimuli are to be kept to a minimum. Communication through body language starts at around four weeks of age along with the first tail wags and puppies will start to claim rank or position within their pack of siblings. They will do this through playing and play-fighting and their position within the pack may change from day to day.

Socialisation falls into three phases. After the imprinting phase mentioned in the previous paragraph comes the true socialisation period. At around 8-12 weeks the puppy will start to recognise people and other canines as fellow-members of its pack and with whom it will form relationships/bonds. If a dog does not have sufficient contact with people between the 3rd and 11th weeks of his life, timidity and fearfulness may be the result and the pup will find it more difficult to develop a bond with humans.

The more contact a dog has in this period with people, with other dogs, other animals and with objects, in short, the more he is involved, the more inclined it will be in later life towards well-balanced behaviour. Smell, touch, skin contact and above all, play, are all of vital importance to a positive mindset and sociable puppy.

The dog must be handled a great deal and have the opportunity to become thoroughly familiar with the scent of humans, male, female, old and young. It is also important that the pup has adequate contact with its own kind to be able to build and maintain communication skills with its own species in the future.

Between now and around 4-5 months is when the young Rottweiler will discover who in this pack is leader. So, any boundaries and rules that have been established will be tested for consistency, and this is a time when you will need to "step up" and support the important structure that has been set in place by you to maintain balance.

By the time your Rottweiler is about 6 months old socialisation must have been maintained and reinforced because whatever is learnt by this stage will remain with the dog into adulthood and throughout its life.

Throughout this period the young Rottweiler should be introduced to as many unfamiliar places as possible as this will help to eliminate undesirable fearful behaviour later on when it is in a place or surroundings that are new to it.

Lack of sufficient exposure to strange or unfamiliar noises can also lead to the Rottweiler becoming hypersensitive upon hearing something it does not recognise. Much of these stimuli can be administered by a knowledgeable breeder but must be continued by you, as pack leader, through sensible acclimatisation.

A puppy that acts fearfully should not be comforted. This will only be seen by the puppy as a sign of weakness or it will confirm the negative state of mind that is being displayed by it. A pack leader would ignore or correct the unwanted behaviours and only give positive attention when the behaviour displayed is desirable. Only give reward for calm submissive behaviour or when your Rottweiler is relaxed. This will encourage a confident, balanced state of being.

Both male and female Rottweilers go through a period of adolescence at between approximately 9 to 36 months. A bitch will have her first season (reproductive cycle) normally between 6 months and 1 year, and this will last for approximately 21 days. Her disposition can be affected by this hormonal change in different ways.

It is important to remember that all of these variants in behaviour should be treated with a calm assertive energy and, where appropriate, she will need to be corrected for any inappropriate behaviour. (It should be taken on board that these variants in her behaviour however, are not a true sign of her temperament). Should you decide not to breed from your female Rottweiler however, she should be spayed about three months after her first season finishes as, at this time, her hormones will likely be back in balance.

During this period of adolescence the male's testosterone levels will also begin to rise, and he will start to lift his leg when urinating. He will start to mark territory when on a walk. He will try to assert himself more with other dogs and humans both those within and outside of your pack. Other signs of adolescence are the testing of boundaries such as not coming when called and a general disobedience. All of these should be handled by correction or consequence and it is important to realize that the youngster is not doing these things with any negative intentions. They are not rationalising the situation and trying to "tick you off". These behaviours are perfectly natural and are a normal part of your dog's development. What is important here is how you, as the leader deal with them?

6. The Needs of a Rottweiler
Will I lead or will I follow?

Leader and Followers

"Leadership gives you control and control gives you leadership"

The Rottweiler has the same psychological needs as any other breed of dog. Sadly to say, as with most "Gladiatorial" breeds, when their needs are not met the outcome can be devastating. A balanced pack structure is therefore extremely important to enable a Rottweiler to be a social domestic animal. It will allow him to be relaxed in any given situation and to be obedient to his pack leader. The Rottweiler is only able to fit into our world using a dog's level of understanding and instinct.

Their instincts are to follow, but only if led by a mentally strong and worthy protector who is calm and assertive and consistent. The challenge for top job will only be tried if weakness is perceived or discovered.

If the Rottweiler is allowed the position of leader above their human companion, they will make decisions based upon their *animal* instincts and not through rational thought, as would a human. This is when problems arise because their instinctual values are <u>not</u> the same as ours.

They will expect you to follow them and they will hand out the discipline when and where they think appropriate. Why? Because you have misguidedly given your dog the job which must be yours!

I always tell people that consistency is important and you must have rules and boundaries. These must be followed at all times, or life will become confused and unpredictable for both you and your Rottweiler.

Making a list of any rules and boundaries and posting them on the fridge door, where everyone can see them is a good reminder for all the family of what is, or isn't, allowed. If you are not consistent with these rules and boundaries then why would you expect your Rottweiler to be?

A Rottweiler needs a firm handler who is fair and dependable, and someone who realises that they must be the leader of their pack. It is a full-time job and you must lead by example, offering guidance and correction when and where necessary. If you are calm, your energy will automatically register with the rest of the pack. Dogs are the masters of body language and they will instinctively pick up your energy and aura and that of your pack. Your Rottweiler will not respect weak energy….and so the most important question you should ask yourself everyday is "In my Rottweiler's eyes, am I a worthy pack leader?"

It is important to remember that a Rottweiler is a working breed and capable of many diverse jobs. It should therefore go without saying that it must have stimulation from its environment and have daily mentally and physically challenging exercise.

The Rottweiler will not thrive in an environment with little or no exercise. If you are not prepared to put in the hard work training and exercising your Rottweiler, this is not the breed for you. While you walk with your Rottweiler, corrections and discipline are part of the pack dynamic and must be administered, by you, as pack leader. If your dog displays a behaviour that you do not agree with, corrections must take place, there and then. Your mental state dictates to the dog whether you are to be taken seriously or not and if you show frustration or impatience when making a correction, you may eventually get your message across, but you will lose the respect and trust that you have worked so hard to acquire. Leadership will give you direct rights to educate your Rottweiler and control the environment in which it lives.

A Rottweiler that has a good bond and trust with its leader will do anything to make them happy. No matter how daft it may be.

7. Learn to understand and be able to think like your Rottweiler.

"Give a Rottweiler the understanding it deserves"

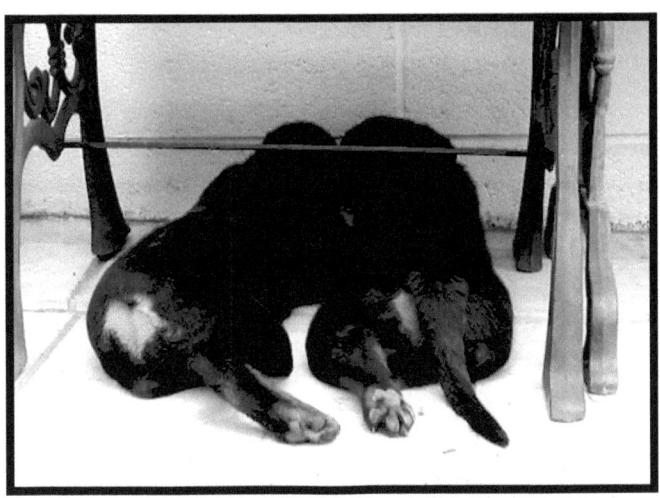

Are these puppies conspiring on how to overthrow the human race?

Learn to understand and be able to think like your Rottweiler. If you can get this right, you are more than half way there.

It is of paramount importance to understand and remember that dogs <u>do not</u> think like people. There is a huge amount of evidence to support the theory that the dog is descended from the wolf, *Canis Lupus*. Regardless of the breed, dogs still display 85% of the natural behaviour patterns exhibited by their ancestors and these are the behaviours of a pack animal. Humans have a very sophisticated brain and ability to reason. A dogs' brain, on the other hand, is smaller and much less complicated. Their first instincts are that of a pack animal.

It is we who put an outer costume on dogs by only breeding for certain strengths or colours, certain forms or functions and then give *this breed* a title.

Your dog's progress is limited only by your time and ability. Your Rottweiler, outside of its animal instincts, is only as clever as you make it! Tell yourself this every day. If you try to think on a dog's level and communicate with him with this in mind, you will be much happier and your pack will naturally find balance.

8. A Dog or a Bitch?

Male and a Female Rottweiler

The decision to choose a male or female should be based upon character, both yours and the Rottweiler's. It is my belief that both sexes can be dominant and disruptive if living in the wrong environment, and with the wrong family.

The breeder that you choose to purchase your Rottweiler from should be able to tell you which sex would suit you and your lifestyle best and give you the reasons for their decision.

If placed in the wrong hands a female Rottweiler with a high intensity is just as much of a liability as a male Rottweiler with the same type of spirit. The biggest difference between male and female apart from the obvious anatomical outer packaging is size and strength, but both sexes have the ability to cause havoc if their needs are not met within their human-canine pack.

Whatever your preference, make sure that you are guided by your head and not by your heart when choosing a Rottweiler puppy, dog or bitch, to invite into your home. Whichever sex you eventually decide on make sure the final choice of pup is for the right reasons.

A puppy that "chose us" is the wrong type of character for an inexperienced home or first time buyer. Equally a pup that excludes itself from introductions and avoids contact would be more suited to someone who has experience and who would know how to give this puppy more confidence. They will be more likely to know how to encourage better social skills after leaving its litter mates.

Someone with a busy family and children would suit a calmer and less pushy pup, one that has confidence but is not "over the top"……and so on.

A good Rottweiler breeder must have this type of knowledge and would want to make sure that your puppy was exactly the right one for you.

Any breeder who lets you come in and choose a puppy without any guidance should be avoided.

9. Rescuing a Rottweiler

Connor is a successful rescue placement. He now lives happily with Jess and Brett. He was originally found wandering the streets.

The rescuing of a Rottweiler is a wonderful act but one that should be thought about carefully before taking the plunge. There are many worthy Rottweilers in rescue centres all over the country, which I am sure will potentially make wonderful additions to a family. These unfortunate animals arrived there through no fault of their own, and may have hidden behaviours that likely have not been disclosed by the person who either abandoned or surrendered them. You must make sure that you go through a registered or knowledgeable charity that will have had the foresight to assess the dog's temperament and social skills before allowing an adoption to take place.

If you decide to go down the rescue route then please remember this:

A Rottweiler would benefit most from a home that will offer it balance and consistency by providing what it needs most - **leadership**. By feeling sorry for the dog because of what may or may not have happened before it found itself in rescue, you will start out by showing a weak mindset and energy and because of this the dog will be unable to move forwards to find balance.

By possibly coming from an unstable existence, the dog will have been under stress permanently and this is an unfair and restrictive state of mind for it to be in. This Rottweiler will <u>not</u> be thinking, "Oh I hope this human will give me loads of treats and cuddles" or "I hope this human doesn't shout at me all the time" a dog doesn't have the ability to justify what may have happened to it in the past. Bad things or inconsistencies may have been experienced in the last pack but what is important to the dog's wellbeing is what is happening in the NOW. They will feel and read you energy, body language and watch your behaviour and so make sure you are displaying that which would be vital to a leader and not a follower.

If you do not show good leadership skills your new pack member will be locked in its past by **you**. A natural consequence of this is that by instinct, the dog may try to take the role of leader and this can cause unnecessary suffering and stress to both human and canine alike.

If you have doubts, go back to the beginning of this book to see clearly what a Rottweiler needs and what makes a good pack leader. All Rottweilers deserve that, surely.

10. Rottweilers and Children.

Educate them both on how they should behave when together!
Blaze with his families Rottweiler puppy Benson are always supervised.

A common question asked is 'are Rottweilers good with children?'

My answer is yes, if children and Rottweilers are socialised and taught how to behave and what is expected of them while in each other's company. A Rottweiler's behaviour will reflect its upbringing.

Like children, a Rottweiler needs consistency and boundaries and as the adult leader in your house it is your job to make sure that before you bring a Rottweiler into your home, you talk to your children about what is expected of them when interacting with their new "friend" and pack member. Once the Rottweiler arrives, supervision is essential so that you can ensure that the environment remains calm and everything goes to plan.

A Rottweiler that has been correctly reared by someone who has ensured that it has had correct introductions to as many children as possible, even if it has been reared in a childless home, will and can interact successfully with children.

Rottweilers that are introduced and taught to respect children as higher ranking than themselves will, and can have an excellent relationship with them. As I have said your Rottweiler will react to every person/child that it meets by using their nose first, which will allow them to assess what the energy/balance of their new pack is. This, in turn, will induce an appropriate reaction by them.

Young children and babies make many different high pitched sounds and erratic movements, all of which to a dog may signify that the child or children are prey or are mentally or physically weakened, and therefore chasing (use of prey instinct) may follow. This is one of the reasons why **interactions with children should always be supervised and introductions ideally done only when the Rottweiler and child are in a calm state of mind.**

Chasing or attacking prey is not always an aggressive act in itself but in fact a very natural response from predator to prey animal. Unless the Rottweiler and children are taught by you to both understand and respect the pack hierarchy and their positions in it, problems can, and will, arise.

When children play they are generally in an excited state of mind and this will encourage the same response in any dog. As mentioned earlier, dogs play in a very different manner while in an excited state of mind.

Interactions must always be supervised where children are concerned and particularly so with children who are very young and do not yet have the capability of fully understanding the consequences of their actions. It is important that you involve all of your family, especially the children, in the supervised education of your Rottweiler pup or adult. By doing this you will be telling the Rottweiler that using respect with this younger and weaker member of your pack is paramount, and anything other than a calm submissive state of mind will not be acceptable and be corrected by you, the ***"Pack Leader"***.

Whatever the relationship your Rottweiler has with children is down to you, not the breed of dog you invite into your home to be a member of your family pack.

These children have wonderful relationships with their Rottweilers.

Part Two

How to be seen as Leader by a Rottweiler.

Rottweilers will always look up to and revere their human or canine leader.

Start as you mean to go on and be consistent with Rules and Boundaries.

1. Control

By controlling your Rottweiler's environment you will be showing it clearly where the boundaries lie. For a Rottweiler to see you as higher ranking, you must show it clearly what is allowed, and what is not. The Rottweiler is living in your home - and not the other way around. You have the duty to say which rooms are accessible, and these rooms should only be entered on your say so. They should only jump up, get on the sofa or bed if you instigate the deed, and most importantly, get off when told to. If it does not, then you must question yourself about the role you have played in this negative response.

If you have decided that you don't like your dog watching you while you are eating, then place him in his bed or a place where he is allowed at every mealtime. If you are consistent with this rule, the dog will eventually leave the room of his own volition when he sees you sit down to eat. A Rottweiler that sits too close and is watching every mouthful that you take is not being respectful and so must be corrected.

A Rottweiler's mother would have corrected this act of "crossing boundaries" when in the litter. Consistency leads to balance and not confusion for the whole pack, dog and human alike.

REMEMBER he's your dog and you have to live with him, so if others say they don't mind him watching them eat, or jumping up uninvited, you must stick to your guns and do not allow it. I could go on and on giving you examples of boundaries but it is up to you, as leader, to decide what you feel is an acceptable demand to make.

"Leadership gives you control and control gives you leadership"

2. Educate the Family

Work as a family unit. Training and balance will be much easier to accomplish if you do.

The whole family should participate in your dog's boundaries, discipline, rules, and, importantly, the praise. Here again consistency is a vital element. The leader should have the responsibility of teaching the family the language and the rules. Ideally this should be done before the puppy comes into the home, so that integration, conditioning and training can begin smoothly.

It will also help if you try to explain to your friends what you expect from them where your Rottweiler is concerned and if they can't or won't do what you would like, take the dog away from the situation so your hard work is not impeded by their apparent lack of support or leadership skills.

(Try making a list of command words with their meanings and posting it on the fridge door, so that everyone can refer to it when in doubt. This can also be done with the rules and boundaries you have decided to implement which must be followed by everyone for the Rottweiler to remain balanced)

3. Patience

Millie being patient, calm and submissive.

Patience - *"The capacity for calmly enduring difficult situations; the ability to wait calmly for something to happen without complaining or giving up"*

Exercise patience with your Rottweiler puppy, as its mother would. If you find yourself becoming impatient, you should take a deep breath or retreat, calm down and closely examine why you have confused the dog. If then the moment is still relevant, try again. If you don't calm down the training process will take much longer and the puppy will become erratic and confused in its behaviour, as it will sense your mood change and weakened energy.

When trying to amend behaviour or change a dog's reactions, be patient and wait for the Rottweiler to be in the right frame of mind before you continue. A mind that is stressed or excited is less efficient in receiving and digesting information.

Remember that the fault lies with us when our dog's behaviour is unacceptable.

4. Walking your Rottweiler

The perfect balance of leader and follower.

It is essential that your Rottweiler has daily exercise in order to ensure a balanced state of mind. The way you start the walk is as important as how you finish it.

Start by making sure your Rottweiler is in a calm submissive state before you set off, as the walk then becomes an incentive and reward for this balanced state of mind. Do not feed an excited state of mind, as anything other than a calm disposition should not be rewarded. You may have to be patient! Use correction for over-excitement and have the dog come to you and sit patiently for its lead to be attached. Each step in this process is a reward in the dog's mind, so think about which state you are encouraging by your actions.

You must also be sure you always go through a doorway or narrow opening first - because you are not the follower. Your Rottweiler will, if it sees you as high ranking, walk with you or behind you, and should only go in front if given your permission.

When I take my dogs for a walk, Rottweiler and Pug alike, I take a walking stick with me. I use this as a vital tool to help maintain control of the pack. The stick is used to touch or block the dog, when I cannot reach with my hand. If used correctly this tool is very useful and quickly respected by the pack when used with the right energy.

I must impress this is not a weapon that should be used to beat the dog with, nor to threaten or intimidate. It is simply an extension of my arm.

Always walk tall with a relaxed calm energy and with an active mind that is watchful, unflappable and composed. This is the energy of a "Pack Leader".

Never let your Rottweiler, whatever its age, off the leash if you are not 100% sure that it will return to you when called.

If your Rottweiler is disobedient within the house or garden when off lead, why on earth do you think it would return to you when other outside stimuli on your walk are far more interesting and distracting than you are? You must start conditioning and showing leadership from the day you bring your Rottweiler into your pack and home if you are at all concerned about safeguarding its welfare.

Letting the dog off the leash too soon is a common mistake made by people who do not put the correct amount of time and effort into training and preparing their dog for interactions outside of the home. If you are in charge and have trained your Rottweiler well, it will return to you promptly as a matter of respect for you, but only if you are a consistent and fair leader.

5. Grooming and Handling

This subject is one that I feel is often neglected when a Rottweiler is purchased. I recommend puppy buyers groom and handle/check a puppy on a daily basis in the beginning because it builds trust and confirms your leadership when done correctly. If you brush and groom your Rottweiler daily and check ears, eyes, nose, teeth/mouth, paws, tail, and underbelly as a matter of your routine it can, and does, prepare your Rottweiler for a number of crucial things, such as a visit to the vet, or removal of something which may have got caught in his paw; most importantly, the dog will learn to place his trust in you as leader and caregiver.

Preferably, while your Rottweiler is young and easier to manage you must insist that it keep still while you do these simple things and you must correct calmly, any fidgeting or struggling that show resentment of being held still. Never release a puppy that is struggling as this tells the pup that *he* controls the situation.

Always exercise patience, as by doing so you are showing control. By the time your Rottweiler has reached six months or so you should be able to do all these things and have complete calm and trust from your puppy.

This is only, of course, if you have been consistent and firm, and haven't caused discomfort or pain while achieving your goal.

When you have reached the point in time when you receive no struggle or resentment from your Rottweiler the procedure will not be necessary so often, but can be carried out whenever you feel it is appropriate.

a) TEETH. When you are checking your dog's mouth and teeth you must be careful that you do not block his airways because this will make him fidget all the more, for obvious reasons. Teeth tend to be the parts of a Rottweiler's daily grooming that most owners neglect. Dogs do not usually get cavities in their teeth, but they can get a build up of tartar. Tartar causes gum disease in dogs just as in humans. Carefully selected diets can help with this problem and also brushing of teeth using specially designed toothpaste and brush can also help. It is cheaper and safer for you to brush your dog's teeth than to have to put him under general anaesthetic for dental procedures. Anaesthesia is always a risk and can be avoided if you just pay attention and keep your canine's teeth pearly white and tartar free.

Your puppy will start to lose puppy teeth at around four months and will have a desire to chew and gnaw to take its mind of this uncomfortable part of its development. Therefore, be prepared for this by supplying him with an acceptable item, such as a hard dog chew or large marrow bone when you cannot keep an eye on things. Do not punish a puppy for trying to cope with teething which is a natural time in development. His teething should be complete by the time he reaches one year, and any baby teeth that may still be in place after this time may need to be removed by a vet.

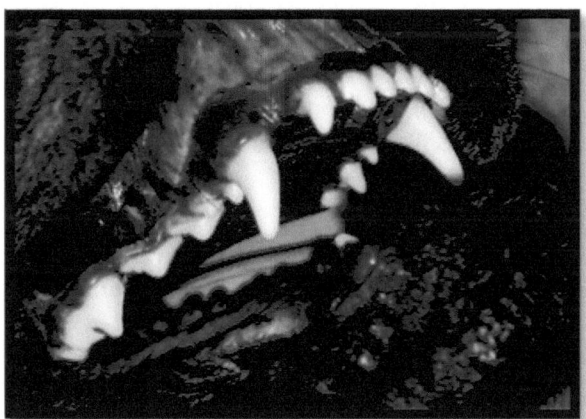

Good clean teeth and a healthy mouth

b) EARS. Ears should be clean and pink inside, with no noticeable odour or secretion. Rottweilers can generate a lot of earwax, and this needs to be removed so that mites, or bacterial or fungal infections, do not move into this inviting warm, moist environment. Never put cotton buds into your dogs' ears but do check them once a month and clean them using a general ear cleanser which can be purchased from any good pet store, your vet's surgery, or on-line. The signs to look for which may tell you something could be wrong and therefore veterinary treatment may be needed are:

1) *Skin within the ear is a colour which is different from the normal skin tone*
2) *Red blotches or scabs from continual scratching*
3) *A strong, unpleasant cheesy or yeasty odour*
4) *Your dog continually shakes its head and scratches its ears.*

c) NAILS. Clipping nails is often forgotten and generally not necessary if your Rottweiler has good tight feet and plenty of exercise on hard surfaces, such as pavements and concrete, as this will help to keep nails short and blunt. If you have never used clippers to cut nails, ask for help from your breeder or perhaps your vet will show you how it is done.

d) EYES. Any discharge from the eyes should be wiped away using a moist tissue or cloth to improve appearance and minimise the chances of infections. Any discharge that is persistent and has colour is a sign of possible infection, and a vet's advice should be sought.

e) COAT. An adult Rottweiler's coat is relatively short and, in general, when not shedding, will need relatively little grooming, perhaps only weekly.

Rottweilers shed their coat twice a year, with males generally shedding once in the spring, and with a lighter shed in the winter.

Females lose their coat before or around their oestrus cycle. (Twice a year)

When the Rottweiler sheds you may find daily grooming necessary for keeping hair in the house down to a minimum and a shedding rake is ideal for this. I also recommend a rubber brush to minimise damage to the skin and which gives your Rottweiler a good massage at the same time as removing unwanted hair.

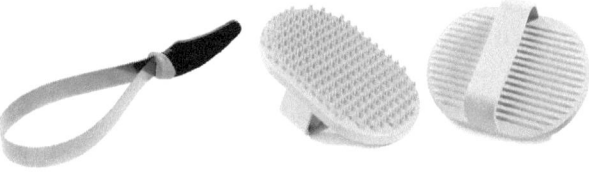

A shedding rake *Rubber hand brush*

Checking other parts of your Rottweilers body is rudimentary and anything which looks or feels or seems out of the ordinary should be examined by your vet.

6. Sharing Affection

Kisses? Not sure I want to!

Sharing affection is enjoyable for both you and your Rottweiler but you must only do so when you want to and not on your dog's instigation. Affection is important for your Rottweiler but it must be in the right context and at the right time. By omitting the correct amount of discipline and giving unbounded amounts of affection you are creating an unnatural and unbalanced state and certainly not one that an Alpha dog would demonstrate to another pack member of lower rank.

A high ranking dog will not give affection to any other pack member unless it wants to, and only on these terms. When a low ranking dog returns to a pack it will automatically lick and submit to the high ranking dog but the high ranking dog will turn its head away. You may ask why? It is because this will be seen as a sign of mental power and strength by its subordinate pack members.

Alpha will not be told when to give affection, when to play, when to hunt or when to sleep, so if your dog comes to you and nudges your arm for a stroke, what should you do? The answer is to ignore the behaviour that is not instigated by you, as leader, and as the higher ranking dog would, until you are ready to show affection on your terms. If you are in the correct state of mind and visualise what you expect from the dog he will pick up on this energy and oblige. Make the dog earn your affection by sitting and staying for a while, or coming when called.

7. Clear Communication

This Rottweiler bitch is calm and submissive. Her eyes are relaxed and her ears held low.

Communication - *"To exchange or make known (information or feelings) by speech, writing or other means."*

Your body language and energy will tell your Rottweiler a lot about you.

The primary communication tool for most humans is our voice but your dog communicates primarily by first using its nose. Sniffing one another's sexual organs or faeces tells them about what the other dog's status is, what sex they are and their maturity and intentions. The dog's posture, eyes, ear position and tail carriage also tells them whether they are dominant, submissive, playful, scared or anxious. Your Rottweiler exchanges information with you in exactly the same way.

Sadly, a dog's effort to communicate with us, as pack members, is quite often misunderstood. This is because many dog owners have not learnt how dogs communicate with one another. They therefore do not possess the ability to translate any clear message which is being shared with them. This same method of communication, use of scent, your energy and your body language is what the dog will use to assess your status and intentions. Your Rottweiler's aims in life are fairly simple: to find leadership, safety, food, and to procreate, but most importantly, to find balance.

As it is clearly not possible for them to learn to speak and understand English, we must, if we want to live safely and experience true friendship with our Rottweiler, learn their language if we are to share "clear communication" with them.

Stress is displaced or displayed too, quite often, by physical self-harm, destruction of your home, chewing things up, excessive barking, heavy panting, restlessness etc. These are all negative behaviours which must be redirected if your dog is to find balance. More exercise and clear communication is what a dog like this needs. A dog that is well balanced will show, in general, a relaxed posture and a calm disposition, with a facial expression to match. Watch your dog and learn from what you see. What do you think he is telling you by his general behaviour and how situations are handled by him? Most importantly how are these situations handled by you?

I once visited a lady who wanted me to help her "*sort out* "her Cocker Spaniel, George. This dog was a sweetheart but manic wasn't the word! He was agitated all the time, panted heavily, eyes wide, tail wagging but low held, he was on the go constantly. The lady said "*he will not come when I call him and he chases everything that comes into the garden and, well, he is like this all the time, oh and he sometimes pees on the kitchen floor*" I will say that this was a lovely family who were by any standard, well off and had a beautiful home. They thought George had everything he wanted. But he didn't have everything that he *needed*.

I ascertained that:

- He wasn't walked daily. The lady thought the garden was big enough for him to run around in.
- George was given frequent cuddles when he demanded them, and because he was "So lovely and cuddly and he loves us".

- No boundaries or rules were in place.
- He had access to the whole of this beautiful mansion which was his to urinate in.

And so my instructions to her, in order for George to find balance, were:

1. Daily exercise, at least 45 minutes once a day or 20 minutes twice a day (at least).
2. Make him earn your affection by waiting for it.
3. Set boundaries and rules in place and make sure he is not allowed through any door before you. Ignore him when you return to a room he is in or when you come home from being out of the house. He should not be acknowledged until he is in a calm state.
4. Stop his access to all rooms in the house except the kitchen and the lounge area, into which he must earn his entry.

I kept in touch with the family on a weekly basis and things were going really well, considering they found it hard not to "love up" this pooch constantly.

Anyway, a month later I had a phone call from the lady saying that she thought that George was depressed! I chuckled to myself and asked her, why?

And wait for it, she said, "Well, every time I come into the room now or I cannot find George because he isn't in the garden chasing the ducks or birds, he's in his bed and just the end of his tail flickers and he doesn't get out of his bed much at all", by this time I am struggling to hold back the laughter and slight frustration as she continued: " I am really worried about him, do you think I need to take him to the vets?"

I said, "No, of course not, this is how he should be. He is relaxed and finally has balance".

The truth is that this lovely lady was so used to seeing this poor dog in a stressed state that she had now decided that *relaxed* meant *depressed* and consequently lifted all boundaries and rules that had helped him find his true place in the pack.

As a result, this poor dog reverted back to the original stressed state I found him in. Some people just don't get it!

8. Corrections and Consequences

Correction - *"to make right and free from error; to conform with expected standards; an act in order to improve"*

Consequence - *"to accept whatever results from ones actions"*

Any negative frame of mind that your Rottweiler displays or any behaviour which in your eyes, as leader, is unacceptable should be redirected using a correction or a consequence……and we now know that this should be done with a calm and assertive manner.

What is meant by correction or consequence? It's fairly simple really. When you are seen as higher ranking, just by looking at your Rottweiler in a disapproving way can get them to stop what they are doing. If you don't have their attention a firm touch with your hand and a strong word such as HEY! Or NO! Will get the result you want, but only if your state of mind is positive. I always think that if you see what you want in your head, it will happen, but if you constantly question yourself, it won't.

If you are walking your Rottweiler, for instance, and he moves too far forwards and tries to take charge of the walk, then use the collar to correct him, jerking the lead to the side and not backwards, along with your chosen sound of disapproval.

If this doesn't work, stop, stand tall, and turn to face him, coolly and calmly walk into the dog until it sits or lies down, and wait until the Rottweiler's posture is calm and submissive, before continuing your walk. This will put you back in charge and tell your Rottweiler that you control the walk.

By now you should know what calm and submissive looks like! Think of how many people you have seen being dragged down the road by a dog and ask yourself next time you see this: Who is the follower in this human-canine pack?

A consequence is an action you enforce for a behaviour that is unacceptable. I would use a consequence if a correction was not working or inappropriate, and the most effective consequence is the opposite of what the dog actually wants.

So if you had visitors and the Rottweiler was being a pest around them and was taking advantage of the weaker, invited pack members (your guests), you should take the dog by the collar and remove it from the room. This should be done in complete silence by you, and with no eye contact made.

For the unacceptable behaviour, your Rottweiler has been banished from the pack by its leader and will only be invited to return when it has reached a calm, submissive and silent state.

This sequence should be repeated until the message is received and understood by your Rottweiler. Some will get the message right away and others may take a little longer to submit to your authority.

9. Praise and Acknowledgement

His first clear jump - what a good boy!

Always praise or acknowledge your Rottweiler's success when teaching new things, when exhibiting good behaviour or when calm and relaxed. This way you will encourage these positive behaviours.

Teaching a Rottweiler tricks or anything new will build confidence, yours and theirs, and will enhance balance in the pack. Only acknowledge what is positive in your eyes as leader and don't focus your attention on anything that is not a required state of mind or behaviour. This might include, for instance, trying to comfort a nervous puppy when it clearly is not in a positive frame of mind. This shows the pup that you agree with or confirm this negative mindset and will not build confidence in the puppy, or its respect for you as leader. When a puppy goes out into the big wide world and sees traffic for the first time it is often a frightening thing for it to deal with and of course, flight would be the pup's option if it weren't for the fact that it is on a lead. This reaction should be ignored and only when the pup is calm and relaxed should attention be given.

If you are in a confident state of mind, relaxed and calm, what energy is your pup picking up on? Always lead by example and don't be tempted to nurture a state of mind that is weak because your Rottweiler will not understand your concern as kindness, but as approval of its state of mind at that moment. Although most pups will eventually get used to traffic, surely it is better to give them a confident leader and not a sympathetic one. Dogs are not sympathetic to one another.

Acknowledge a state of mind that will be productive and not destructive. Praise your Rottweiler for doing things well and embrace this spirit.

10. Playtime

Early retrieve taught as a very young puppy can be turned into a structured exercise when older.

Playtime is a time to teach good pack social skills and should be instigated by you as pack leader. When dogs play they use their mouths and bodies to wrestle and chase one another. When in a litter, Rottweiler pups will learn bite inhibition when playing by biting each other and when a bite is too hard and it hurts, a shrill squeak will be heard and then a refusal to play, or a scrap, may start. This will be over quickly and play begins again.

On the other hand, if a pup chews on mum's ear or thinks mum's paw looks good to munch on, she will growl or push the pup away, the severity of which will only be heightened by her if the pup doesn't get the message first time. So when the Rottweiler comes into a human pack they have to learn how to play with respect - and your role as leader is vital here. The more excitable the game is, the more excitable the Rottweiler is, and so on. Use playtime to teach a retrieve, leave and take the toy or "find it" games, these are just as much fun for the Rottweiler as rough and tumble, which I do not advise unless you are experienced and training for a particular purpose. Rough and tumble and tug of war are power games and may encourage your Rottweiler to challenge you inappropriately.

It is a good idea to keep toys under your control as leader and the dog should only have access to them when you say so. The reasons for this are:

a) They are pack leader's toys and you ultimately control them.

b) If freely available they will lose their value to your Rottweiler and become less exciting. This means they won't be as rewarding when used as a prize in training.

c) Rottweilers have very powerful jaws and can chew through many things, all of which we do not want swallowed.

A calm and submissive Rottweiler pup

11. Pack Dynamics

In a pack there are various roles to be filled and the most important is "Leader": YOU.

You should control everything in your Rottweiler's eyes and he must follow and obey. You are responsible for his food, his water, his well-being, his safety, his warmth, his shelter, his grooming and his LIFE. The higher up in the pack you are, the more privileges you are allowed. Sounds simple right?

If you have a multiple dog household, the only rank that you should worry about maintaining is yours. The other canine pack members should be allowed to communicate with each other to keep themselves in their order of hierarchy.

The only time I step in to diffuse a situation is when I feel it is getting too heated and I then just step between them, project disapproval, calmly, and they will move away and go on about their business. Needless to say this only works if you have a balanced pack and your Rottweiler respects you.

Before we can start to overcome problem behaviour, or even contemplate training our dogs, we should ensure that the dog views its position within our pack as being lower ranking than we humans. And for the social structure of the pack to hold together, it must have a leader or Alpha figure, and this must be YOU.

Here are some non-confrontational ways to achieve leadership:

1. Deny your Rottweiler freedom of movement around the house. Only allow entry to rooms on your say so.

2. Feed your Rottweiler after you have eaten. This instinctively tells the dog that at meal times you get the best and he gets the rest.

3. Only play competitive games like tug of war if you are prepared to win them. These games should be started by you and ended by you. This means that you must also maintain control of the toys, and put them away when you have had enough and while your Rottweiler is still keen.

4. Always go through doors, gates or narrow openings before your Rottweiler. Make the dog follow you, not lead or push you through.

5. If your Rottweiler is in your way use your body to move him out of the way, if he doesn't move voluntarily. If one of my dogs positions himself in the doorway trying to go through first, I step across and in front, blocking his way. It is *my* door! If there is respect the dog will move happily.

6. Any behaviour that your Rottweiler displays that is inappropriate must be redirected using a correction or a consequence.

Never treat or think of your Rottweiler as if he were human, this will be undermining his real identity as an animal and is one of the most common mistakes made by well-meaning humans.

There are some Rottweilers to which none of the above is applicable and problems are never experienced. Although, I must say, that depends on what you may or may not find offensive or acceptable in your pack.

My grandparents for example, were dominated by their Yorkshire terrier, who would not let them out of the house to go shopping or let them groom him, plus many other outrageous behaviours but they seemed to think was just his 'personality'. If you've been following closely, I think you will have worked out who was the leader in their house and who were the followers.

What has been written above may seem harsh and perhaps, to you, unnecessary but please remember that your Rottweiler's identity is *animal first*. You can give him the best of everything in your eyes, but in his eyes the best you can give is a strong, confident, reliable and fair leader, who admires him for what he truly is, a magnificent Rottweiler, a breed of dog which has strength, ability and beauty, only when led by a strong and worthy Pack Leader.

The Look of Calm Submission is also a feeling of Calm Submission

The face of a well balanced, calm and relaxed puppy called Benson

And the same state of mind in an adult called Niko.

12. Aggression

A Rottweiler is not born aggressive or with aggressive tendencies. It will learn these behaviours by what it may or may not experience before and after leaving a litter. This means that we have the power to control this negative state of mind. A Rottweiler can learn to use aggression to repel that which it fears or to use dominance to achieve submission from a possible threat or weaker energy. This is a natural reaction or instinctual behaviour for a dog to use when it hasn't been understood and nurtured by us correctly.

"Prevention is better than cure", by making sure a Rottweiler, puppy or adult, has the correct balance within its lifestyle and surroundings. Through this we can ensure that it will never have to show any unnecessary aggression towards us or within its environment.

As a guarding breed the Rottweiler, naturally will be more predisposed to what we may describe as *"aggression"*, which is in fact a result of a learnt reaction to a certain event or situation or use of a natural instinctual behaviour. (See **Understanding the Rottweiler's Instincts** on page 6). When not in a balanced home, one where the most senior component is not the human, the Rottweiler may feel a stronger need to be territorial and/or dominant in its surroundings, which, I might add, is a perfectly natural behaviour for any canine, when the role of leader is not already taken by a human. So it is very important that you are in control and do show consistency with the boundaries and rules within the "pack".

In a dog's world they would have a pack order which determines their social status and the amount of privileges that they may have. This order is maintained and kept using discipline and corrections, when boundaries and rules are broken or crossed.

The *Alpha* or *leader* position must always be ours when Rottweilers live with us. They look at us as members of the pack and try to establish their position in it by challenging our authority, and this usually starts with the weaker or more submissive pack members, who are often children.

When a Rottweiler is a puppy and tries to naturally challenge us by growling, perhaps when we approach its food, or a toy, the pup *must* be corrected. If we allow this to go unchallenged, it will allow the Rottweiler pup to gain status within the pack structure and will become a behaviour which will only intensify and become more difficult to correct as the Rottweiler gets older and stronger.

It is my belief that a Rottweiler, or any other canine put into a leadership role – an impossible task for a dog in a domestic environment - is a dog under a huge amount of stress.

This burden is created by unsuspecting, well meaning people who think you only need "love" to raise a Rottweiler. A person who gives unrestrained amounts of affection, unearned privileges and treats for free and the most comfortable chair in the house whenever it is desired will have set the road to disaster.

It takes a lot more than love to raise a well balanced and trustworthy Rottweiler. You need to have a good understanding of what makes a canine's life balanced and relaxed. Dogs have no conception of what humans see as "love". When love is given from a human perspective, what you are actually showing is weakness to your Rottweiler. Replace the word "love" with "affection" and give it at the right time, the time when the dog displays the correct frame of mind and good behaviour.

On the other hand, a Rottweiler that is left to its own devices and with little or no positive mental or physical fulfilment is likely to use "aggression" to get a message across because it is frustrated or dominant within its environment.

Aggression can also manifest itself in a Rottweiler that is not correctly socialised with other dogs or people, where the dog believes it is dominant and tries to use assertive behaviour with them. This Rottweiler may also develop a fear or nervous aggression when around strangers or unfamiliar dogs and the fight or flight option is not available to them.

If you dictate your Rottweiler's state of mind - which should be calm and submissive, by using the correct tools to communicate with them, you are very unlikely to see a Rottweiler use aggression. The use of aggression for a Rottweiler is a last resort, used when all its attempts to get a message across have failed.

Guarding is part of the Rottweiler's heritage and should be understood fully by you and not forced in any way to promote this breed as unstable. As a working breed they are intelligent and friendly and very trainable if you take the time and effort to discover correctly their potential as a companion, show dog or working partner. Your Rottweilers behaviour will be a reflection of your knowledge and hard work or sadly not, as the case often is.

A recipe for disaster is any person who does not think further than the outer packaging of the breed and the person who takes advantage of the breed's vulnerability as a *"status symbol"*. Someone who has not considered whether they are able to give this breed the correct amount of positive input, mentally and physically, should never be allowed the privilege of living alongside this magnificent breed of canine "The Rottweiler".

If your Rottweiler is using aggression or has aggressive tendencies, I urge you to find a professional dog trainer to work with you and your dog. Do not allow the problem to escalate, because it is the Rottweiler that pays the ultimate price in the end and the rest of us who are working to save this breed are labelled because of it. Most cases are the owners' lack of knowledge about canine language and how they should and must be seen by their Rottweiler.

Time to Decide

By now I would hope that this book will have helped you decide whether the Rottweiler is the right breed for you and your family and give you a clear image of what and does go very wrong. So if you are:

- Willing to offer a Rottweiler leadership, consistency and fulfilment.
- Willing to offer a stable environment with all the relevant aspects of life that enables a Rottweiler to be balanced.
- Authoritative, patient and level headed.
- New to the breed, and you are still eager to learn more.

This means you have some of the essential qualities to make responsible and caring Rottweiler owner.

I also hope that if you already have a Rottweiler and things are not on track, this book may have helped you to work out where you have gone wrong and how you may be able to rectify the problems. It will hopefully prompt you to seek professional help to give your Rottweiler what he really deserves, balance, your leadership and ultimately your protection.

Other Tools You Will find Useful

Apart from the usual collar and lead and a ready food source I would recommend the follow items for use with a Rottweiler.

A collapsible crate is very useful

A large crate is useful because it helps with house training by restricting the puppy's freedom when you are unable to continue toilet schedules, like at night time. It keeps a puppy safe from mischief when you are unable to supervise. It is also a secure place for your Rottweiler to use as a place to relax or you may find it useful when your Rottweiler may be recovering from an injury or operation which warrants restricted movement.

Stainless Steel bowls are hygienic and long lasting. Recommended bowl size is 10 inches, one for water and one for food.

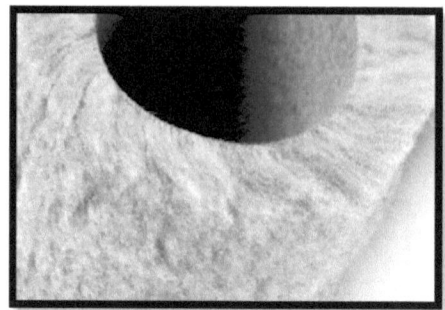

The bedding which I recommend is original Vetbed. It is still the UK's and possibly the world's leading veterinary pet bedding because it is:

- Very long lasting
- Machine washable – over and over again at up to 90°C
- Thicker pile – for greater heat retention
- Double woven – makes it harder to chew
- Portable – use it at home or when travelling
- Hygienic – non irritant and non-allergic
- Recommended by vets – the beds they use the most
- Drains and dries fast – keeps your pets warm and dry even if accidents occur

It can be purchased from local pet shops and some veterinary clinics but most cheaply over the internet and comes in a very wide range of colours. Now also with a non- slip backing to limit movement on slippery surfaces.

My Rottweiler's Personal Information.

(Temperature of a dog, *canis lupus* 38.3°C or 101.50°F)

Rottweiler's Call Name	
Breeder's Details	
KC Registration Name	
KC Registration No.	
Date of Birth.	
Microchip or Tattoo No	
Insurance Details.	
Vets Details	

Weight *(AV approx adult)* Males *app*rox 50kg Females *approx* 42kg	
Vaccination Date	
Booster Date	
(F) Season dates	

NOTES

Other Recommended Reading

Think Dog by John Fisher ISBN *0 71372568 0*

Why Does My Dog by John Fisher ISBN *0 28563058 X*

Clicker Training by Karen Prior ISBN *1 86054 2824*

The Dog Listener by Jan Fennell ISBN *0 00 257204 4*

The Practical Dog Listener by Jan Fennell ISBN *0 00 257205 2*

Be the pack Leader by Cesar Millan and Melissa Jo Peltier ISBN *978-0-307-38166-8*

Cesar's Way by Cesar Millan with Melissa Jo Peltier ISBN *978 0 340 933176*

Give Your Dog a Bone by Dr Ian Billinghurst ISBN *0 646 16028 1*

Grow your Pup with Bones by Dr Ian Billinghurst ISBN *0 9585925 00*

The Barf Diet by Dr Ian Billinghurst ISBN *0 9585925 19*

Raw meaty Bones by Tom Lonsdale ISBN *0646 39624 2*

Living with the Rottweiler by Kate Pinches ISBN *1 86054 168 2*

Quebex Canine Prints and Cards

Above some of our artwork and cards that can be purchased from our online shop.

www.canineprintsandcards.quebex.co.uk

In our shop you will find a wonderful range of cards for any time of year which are excellent value for money and totally original. Our prints are 8 by 10 inch in size and are mounted with high quality mounts sealed with a back board to make sure they remain in mint condition. They are ready for framing in a 10 by 12 inch frame and make excellent gift at any time of year.

You can expect to receive a friendly and reliable service and items of excellent value and quality.

Show support for this Wonderful Breed

By joining

ROTTWEILER OWNERS' TRUST

Misrepresented, Misunderstood ......but Magnificent.

www.rottweilerownerstrust.synthasite.com

Through joining this Trust, Members will be part of a national network of people who are prepared to stand up and defend the Rottweiler.

www.rossmccarthy.com

Ross McCarthy **MBIPDT MCFBA MGoDT (MT)**

Ross and his colleagues see many breeds of dogs who display countless types of inappropriate behaviour of varying degrees and intensity. It is disheartening that in the majority of cases, these problems could have been prevented through correct, species appropriate rearing, the implementation of consistent boundaries and sensible obedience training.

Coalition for Improved Dog Ownership Standards

www.cfidos.co.uk

The Coalition for Improved Dog Ownership Standards (C-fidos) is a non profit organisation established as an affiliate partner of the Pet Owners Parliament.

Aims and Objectives

The 7 Founding Principles of C-fidos:

1) That dogs and society in the UK would benefit from a nation of better informed dog owners

2) That dog related legislation should be fair and not based on breed type

3) That the UK should strive to address and reduce the number of dogs surrendered to shelters

4) That all dog owners should be made aware of the principles of the Animal Welfare Act

5) That all potential dog owners should be better informed as to how to select responsible suppliers of dogs

6) That irresponsible suppliers and producers of dogs should be properly legislated against

7) That educating young people about dogs is to the great benefit of dogs and society in the future

If you agree with the founding principles of C-fidos you may wish to join us as a supporter or a member of our steering group.

www.ingramcontent.com/pod-product-compliance
Ingram Content Group UK Ltd.
Pitfield, Milton Keynes, MK11 3LW, UK
UKHW041434180426
11947UKWH00007B/434